HEINKEL
He 162
"Volksjäger"

Heinz J. Nowarra

SCHIFFER MILITARY HISTORY
Atglen, PA

Cover Artwork by Steve Ferguson, Colorado Springs, CO

THE SPARROW FROM ROSTOCK

In the deparate days of February 1945, the Luftwaffe pressed the He 162 "Spatz" (Sparrow) into service with one of the most experienced Reich Home Defense gruppen on the Western Front — JG 1 "Oesau" based at Parchim. After two convoluted months of reorganization and treacherous training flights with the unproven "Volksjäger", Gruppen Kommodore Obst. Herbert Ihlefeld declared I./JG 1 operational with twenty-five 162s at Leck airdrome on the Danish border. The first official missions were flown on 21 April against Allied ground forces.

Despite overwhelming vulnerability to the Allies' 2nd Tactical Air Force, only one He 162 of I/JG 1 was lost to enemy action. In contrast, the Gruppe claimed two victories, but the record details are not clearly defined. By using the 4 May mission reference and existing photos, it is reasonable to display the "White 1" with its adopted JG 77 eagle badge as the He 162 in which Lt. Rudolf Schmitt shot down an RAF Typhoon near Rostock, Germany, the very town where Heinkel workers has assembled "White 1" in late 1944. Four days after Schmitt's aerial victory, Obst. Ihlefeld ordered his Sparrows grounded. The war was over in Europe.

Sources:
— Factory files of the Heinkel firm
— *Jetplanes of the Third Reich*, Smith-Creek
— *Ritterkreuzträger der Luftwaffe*, Obermeier
Photographic acknowledgements:
— NSM Smithsonian Institution (color photo on rear cover)
— VFW, Bremen
— Armin Kerle, Böblingen
— Peter Petrick, Berlin
— Nowarra archives

Translated from the German by James C. Cable.

Printed in the United States of America.
ISBN: 0-88740-478-2

This title was originally published under the title,
Der "Volksjäger" He 162",
by Podzun-Pallas Verlag, Friedberg.

We are interested in hearing from authors with book ideas on related topics. We are also looking for good photographs in the military history area. We will copy your photos and credit you should your materials be used in a future Schiffer project.

Published by Schiffer Publishing, Ltd.
77 Lower Valley Road
Atglen, PA 19310
Please write for a free catalog.
This book may be purchased from the publisher.
Please include $2.95 postage.
Try your bookstore first.

We are interested in hearing from authors
with book ideas on related subjects.

Ernst Heinkel after the war with a model of the He 162.

Heinkel He 162, The "Volksjäger"

On 10 July 1944 the leader of the Heinkel Projects branch, Siegfried Günter, presented his report 105/44 titled "P 1073 Jet Fighter" to the appropriate leadership of the factory in Rostock and Vienna. This document maintained, among other things, "the achievement of air superiority is dependant not only upon the number of single-seaters but also upon the speed of the single-seat fighter. Should enemy jet single seat fighters be deployed, the Me 262 could probably not be counted on for air superiority, because its conventional construction with unswept wings and the placement of its engine nacelles give too much resistance — at low altitudes its fuel expenditure is quite large and its range quite small. For these reasons, it is necessary to concentrate on a single-seat aircraft with the least possible amount of equipment and not limit fuel to so small a portion of the overall weight." Günter had calculated the following performances of his P 1073 project with two different engines:

— with the Heinkel He S 11 (still in development)

maximum speed	1,010 km/h
range with normal fuel tanks	1,000 km
with drop tanks	1,650 km

— with the Jumo 004 C

maximum speed	940 km/h

Siegfried Günter, spiritual father of the He 162.

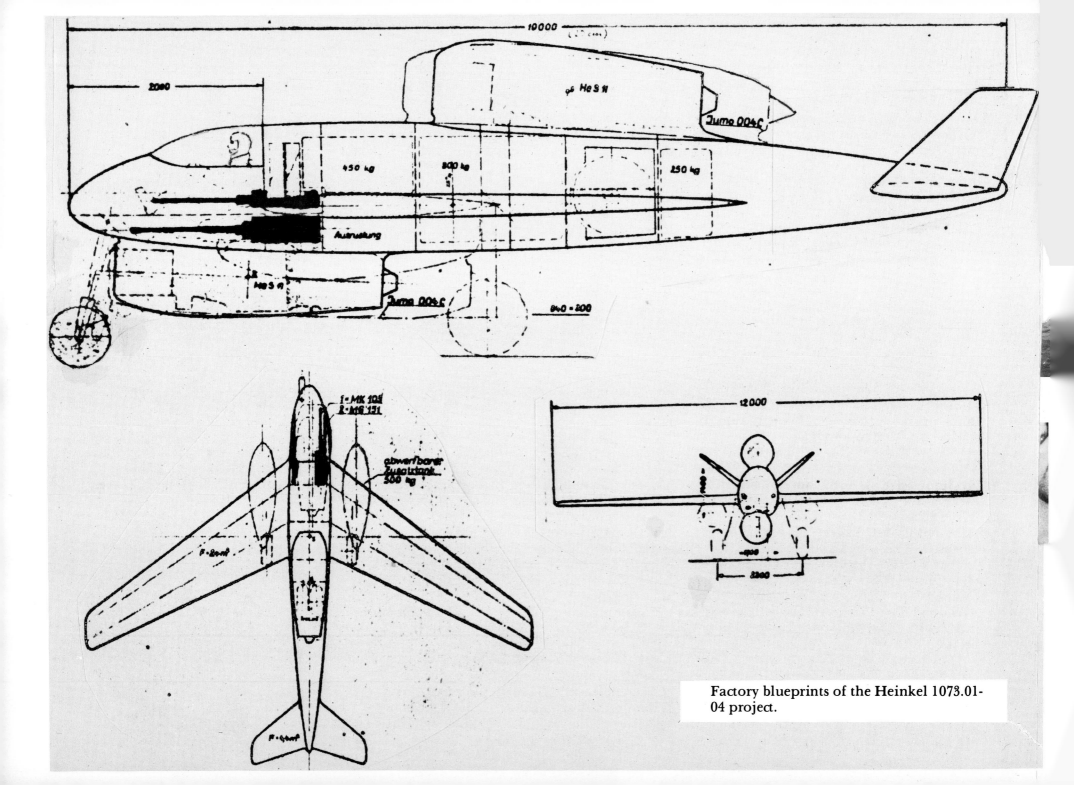

Factory blueprints of the Heinkel 1073.01-04 project.

The model with the HeS 11 was to go into production as the He 500 A, and that with the Jumo 004 C as the He 500 B.

The discussion at Heinkel about this project was still going on when, on 8 September 1944, the *Reichsluftfahrtministerium* (RLM) (Reichs Ministry for Air Transport) invited bids from Blohm & Voss, Focke-Wulf, Heinkel and Junkers for a jet fighter and engine.

The Heinkel people got moving right away on this, returned to Günter's P 1073 project, changed the plans to correspond to the RLM requirements and submitted plans P.1073-01-18 and P.1073-01-20 by 11 September, both, however, now with BMW 003A-1 engines.

Focke-Wulf and Junkers turned down the contract. Only Arado presented its E.580 plans on schedule. Then came a P.210 project from Blohm & Voss, which was followed by an improved P.211 on 15 September. The following notes were made about the discussion at the RLM on this day:

"Take-off roll requirement: a take-off roll of 500m not attainable. Arado and Heinkel are impressive in form and construction; inexpensive and expedient. Construction materials are chiefly wood and steel. Because these points best reflect the requirements, this aircraft must be built.

"Drawings of the plans must be delivered two months after the awarding of the contract. The maiden flight is to take place two months thereafter. The *Reichsmarschall*'s decision is in favor of the Heinkel project.

"The demands of this tight schedule can only be met by the Ernst-Heinkel-Flugzeugwerke because this factory has the available free capacity."

The Arado design was rejected from the outset. In the basic concept the E.580 was similar to the later He 162. The main difference was the type of construction of the low wing. The main material was wood, and the planned engine was the BMW 003A-1 with 700 kp (kilograms thrust). The fuel was contained in two tanks with a capacity of 250 liters each, the engine, as with the He 162, mounted on the back of the aircraft. The lesser power output than that of the He 162 as well as the B & V project P.211 led to the rejection.

The competing design from B & V was essentially developed from three designs. This, too, approached the problem of the *Volksjäger* in a step-by-step fashion. It was basically designed around a tubular all-steel mounting from which the engine was slung behind the cockpit and served as the mount for the rudder as well. A second thinner tubular construction was the basis for the wing.

The elevator assembly formed an isosceles triangle, the rudder an oblique-angled triangle. The armament was to consist of two MK 108 cannons, whose firing ports were located to the left and right of the jet engine intake. The air was channeled under the pilot seat through a tunnel to the BMW 003 jet engine located behind the pilot's seat. The exhaust port was located under the empannage. The measurements were as follows:

wingspan	8.38 meters
length	8.68 meters
height	2.66 meters

With a takeoff weight of 2,758.8 kilograms the aircraft was supposed to be able to reach a maximum speed of 760 km/h at ground level, and 857.6 km/h at an altitude of 7,500 meters.

The rate of climb was calculated to be 100 meters per minute near ground level, while at 7,500 meters it was only 370 meters per minute. It was able to achieve a take-off roll of 750 meters from a combat grass airstrip and a 640 meter take-off roll from a concrete runway. Wood and steel were planned as the primary construction materials, steel making up 58 percent, wood 23 percent, duraluminium 13 percent and the remaining six percent from synthetic materials. In contrast to the He 162, the landing gear could be partially retracted into the wings. The tires lay flat in a collar under the turbine. The nosegear was turned 90 degrees when being retracted so that it, too, would lie flat against the fuselage nose. The tubular shaped wing also acted as a fuel tank together with the same kind of tubing of the fuselage. Fuel capacity was about 700 liters, which gave a range of about 1,000 kilometers. Maximum altitude was 18,000 meters.

On 19 September, a meeting chaired by *Generalingeneur* Lucht took place at the technical bureau of the RLM in which the following firms to part: Arado, Blohm & Voss, Focke Wulf, Fiesler, Junkers, Siebel, Heinkel.

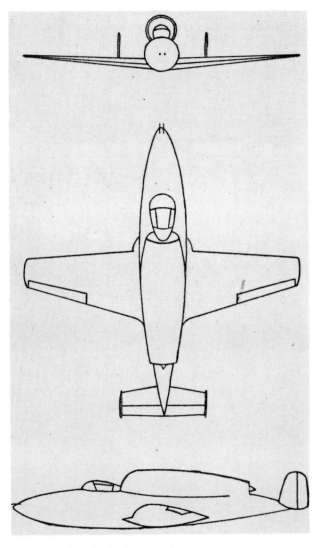

Arado E.580 project.

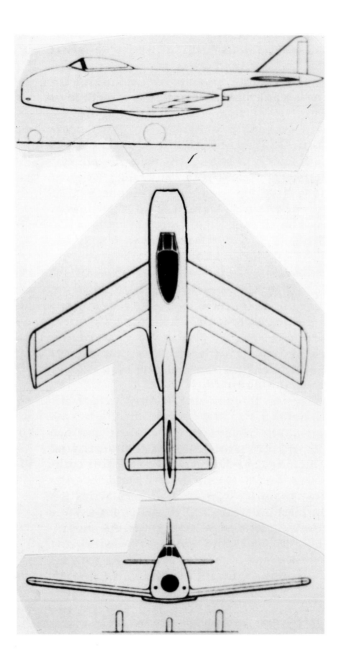

Blohm & Voss project 211 (Dr. Vogt).

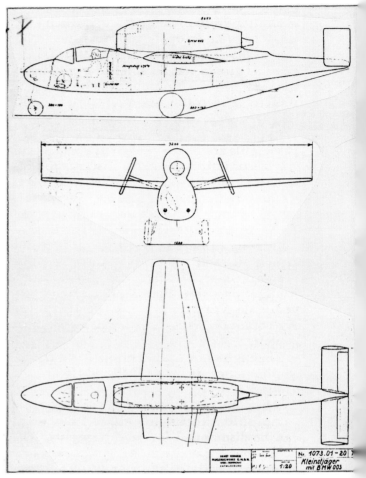

Heinkel project 1073.01-20 (closely corresponds to the He 162 V1).

All of the firms, except Heinkel and B & V, submitted drafts of new projects, which were declined after in-depth testing. The Siebel project was commented on only briefly, the Heinkel project was accepted outright, without comparative study against the B & V project. The following points had to be emphasized:

1. Weights according to the requirements of the Technical Bureau. No discernable differences from the Heinkel project. The aerodynamic performance of the B & V projects is in all realms of flight equivalent, or even better as a result of the sufficient lack of interfering surfaces.
2. The airframe weight is not heavier. The 30kg difference cited is within the allowable limits of precision, that is it lies within non-verifiable accuracy.
3. Visibility is better than that of the Heinkel project.
4. The engines are easily installed or removed. Maintenance is accomplished from the ground.
5. Dismantling and assembly can be accomplished with simple tools, and the aircraft can be dismantled for road transport. The additional expenditure of work time and complexity of the wing dismantling points is offset by the robust right-angle wings. Standard rail cars can be used for rail transport. In this case, only the outer surfaces are taken off.
6. A higher state of combat readiness is possible compared to the Heinkel project due to the simplified Maintenance procedures.
7. Extensively reduced use of scarce materials. The steel sheeting is used in such a way that no uncomfortably thin or weak areas in the fuselage are to be observed.
8. The time needed for the inevitable overhaul is unusually short.
9. The demand of production materials is workable and slight.
10. The actual production requirements including assembly is less than any method of construction suggested up to this point.

During the meeting, there was no discussion of sincerely testing the B & V project. Heinkel's general director Frydag doubted the advantages of the methods of construction and considered the use of removable areas of fuselage skin to be elaborate and difficult. The B & V project received nothing but criticism, the economic advantages were ignored.

The decision for the project now called the *Volksjäger* was postponed. Further talks in Hamburg were supposed to clarify new proposals. Playing a decisive role in this delay is the modest expenditure of production materials and a production time of only 1,600 hours for one aircraft.

Despite all objections by Dr. Vogt (of B & V) Heinkel received the contract. *General-Ingenieur*s Lucht and Saur, the *Jägerstab* Chief of Staff, were convinced that the engine installation in Vogt's P.211 was too complicated. Four weeks later, even Professor Messerschmitt expressed opinions against the Heinkel project. Heinkel promptly rejected Messerschmitt's opinions. As always, work was accomplished very quickly at Heinkel and the complete construction description of the He 162 was finished on 15 October 1944. Two days later, the final discussion between the gentlemen of the *Technisches Amt* and from the Heinkel firm took place.

Final form of the He 162 A.

December 10th, 1944 was named as the date for the completion of the first prototype, the He 162 V 1. Things went quickly at Heinkel and *Flugkapitän* Peter was able to take off on the maiden flight as early as December 6th.

On the day of the original production deadline, the 10th of December, a catastrophe occurred: during a test flight, with ten degrees inclination, the He 162 V 1 crashed from an altitude of 100 meters with a speed of about 700 km/h and unusually quick roll movements to the right. The right wing tip had come off, as had the right aileron. *Flugkapitän* Peter died in the crash. Nevertheless, work continued as they could definitely determine the cause of the accident: poor assembly, weak nose ribbing, improper material for parts of the aileron assembly, etc.

On 22 December, He 162 V 2 was ready for its maiden flight, which would be conducted by *Direktor* Francke, the former test pilot from Rechlin and now director at Heinkel.

Above: Heinkel He 162 V 1. Serial number 200001.

Below: *Flugkapitän Diplom Ingeneur* Peter together with his wife Helga and factory pilot Adolf Fach (right), flew the He 162 in Lechfeld.

Left: Ernst Heinkel and Karl Schwärzler, chief of the Construction Bureau, observe the maiden flight of the He 162.

Below left and right: Photos of the doomed flight of the He 162 V on December 10, 1944 from a film taken by *Leutnant* Helmut Kudliche of the RLM film department.

Above: Peter attempted to make a low-level pass.

Above: During an overflight of the observers, the right aileron began to come apart.

Below: At the same time, wing's leading edge began to disintegrate.

Below: Then the aircraft plummeted and smashed to bits.

No severe complications arose. The V 3 and V 4 were also ready by 16 January 1945. Testing began right away. In the meantime, mass production was run up.

Thirty-four fuselages were built in Rostock-Marienehe by the 20th of January 1945. It became apparent, however, that the wood construction elements manufactured by subcontractors had to be strengthened and reworked. A *Meister*, a foreman and 20 specialist carpenters had to be hired for this purpose. When one takes into account that at this point in time the entire air transport industry and the German traffic network was suffering under constant day and night attacks by Allied aircraft, one must consider the work done by the Heinkel factory to be quite extraordinary.

Construction of the V 2 and V 3 began on the 22nd and 23rd. On 27 January, Heinkel (Rostock) reported the the planned output of 30 He 162's in January 1945 was not possible. The reasons for this have already been discussed above. Individual parts, which were produced in a decentralized system, did not arrive. Aside from this it became clear that the wings had to be strengthened. Francke ordered that the first mass-produced aircraft were not to be flown at speeds above 500 km/h.

On 28 January 1945 the He 162 V 5 was also ready, which then received the nomenclature He 162 A-01 as the first mass-produced model. Francke gave a detailed report on 30 January about the flight characteristics of the He 162 as ascertained by him, in particular those which led to changes to the tail assembly and to the wings.

Production of the individual main components of the He 162 was accomplished aside from other suppliers in the underground former chalk mine "Languste" which

Diplom Ingeneur Francke, still a Luftwaffe officer, with Ernst Heinkel and retired Admiral Lahss. In the right foreground is Siegfried Günter.

was located in Mödling near Vienna. The following were intended for final assembly: Heinkel-North (Rostock-Marienehe), Heinkel-South ("Languste") and Junkers in Bernburg. The serial numbers for the aircraft from Rostock began with 120, those from "Languste" with 220 and those from Junkers in Bernburg with 300. Later, central factory in Nordhausen was to produce aircraft whose serial numbers were to start with 310. It seems these production centers did not come into fruition.

He 162 parts manufacture in the "Languste" underground plant in Mödling near Vienna.

On February 4, He 162 A-02 crashed on its eleventh flight. It turned out that the He 162 had a tendency to nosedive over its wing, which made further changes necessary. Despite this, Francke gave a basically positive report about the He 162, but did not touch upon pitch stability. On the same day, Rostock reported that two He 162's were flight operational, twelve were ready for engine testing, 71 fuselages were finished and a further 58 fuselages were in the initial stages of assembly. Three days later, during its 18th factory flight, an He 162 V made an off-airfield landing which resulted in 40% damage.

On 11 February the *General der Jagdflieger, Oberst* Gordon Gollob and *Oberstleutnant* Walther Dahl, as well as two gentlemen from the Rechlin testing facility, were briefed on the state of the He 162 production. As such, it was determined that aircraft could not be available for deployment until the second half of April at the earliest. At the end of February one *Staffel* from II/JG 1 was to be set to Vienna in order to familiarize them with the He 162 delivered from the "Languste" facility. I/JG 1 in Parchim was to be outfitted with those aircraft manufactured in Rostock and Bernburg. The only complaint was about the poor range of the FuG 24 radio. Gollob insisted on further production installations of variometers and gun cameras. On 15 February 1945, Professor Lippisch, who up to this point had been working in Vienna, offered to work on the suggested improvements to the He 162, but this was not to be.

On February 28 1945 the *Jägerstab* implemented an emergency plan for fighters in which the following production prototypes were to be built: Blohm & Voss P 212, Focke-

Wulf Ta 183/I and Ta 183/II, Heinkel P.1078, Junkers EF 128 and the projects from Messerschmitt, the 1101, 1110 and 1111. But the only one built was a mockup of the Me P.1101 which was later brought to the U.S. and tested. All of the other projects could be developed no further.

In the mean time, other people had become interested in the *Volksjäger* project. Hitler had received information by 25 September 1944 about a unit of the SS which was to be equipped with the *Volksjäger*. The leader of the national socialist *Fliegerkorps* at the time, the former chief of *Luftflotte 1*, *Generaloberst* Alfred Keller, got wind of this and summoned the *Reichsjugendführer* and suggested to Göring that the *Volksjäger* aircraft, which was to have a production run in the thousands, all be flown by the glider pilots of the Hitler Youth. A corresponding training unit was actually set up in Trebbin for this purpose. Engineless He 162's were delivered there and flown in tow by Hitler Youth pilots. Further war developments prevented one of the Hitler Youth pilots from ever having to fly the He 162, which, in view of the situation, could only have led to deadly consequences.

The Luftwaffe had already established an He 162 testing unit under the leadership of Heinz Bär, first in Rechlin-Roggenthin, then in Lechfeld. Assignment of ground personnel took place after their training at the *Fliegertechnische Schule 6* at Neuenmarkt and Weidenberg near Bayreuth. Under command of *Oberst* Ihlefeld, I/JG 1 began its training with help from factory pilots. Ihlefeld went, as far as is known, together with his staff to Lechfeld for further deployment testing. According to testimony of his wingman Sill, he is said to have achieved an aerial victory

There were additional underground facilities in a salt mine in Eger near Salzburg.

Generaloberst Keller (left) with Fr. W Siebel and *Oberst* Beckmann in Trebbin.

Generaloberst Keller in conversation with a member of the SS.

Right side: Factory overview plans of the He 162.

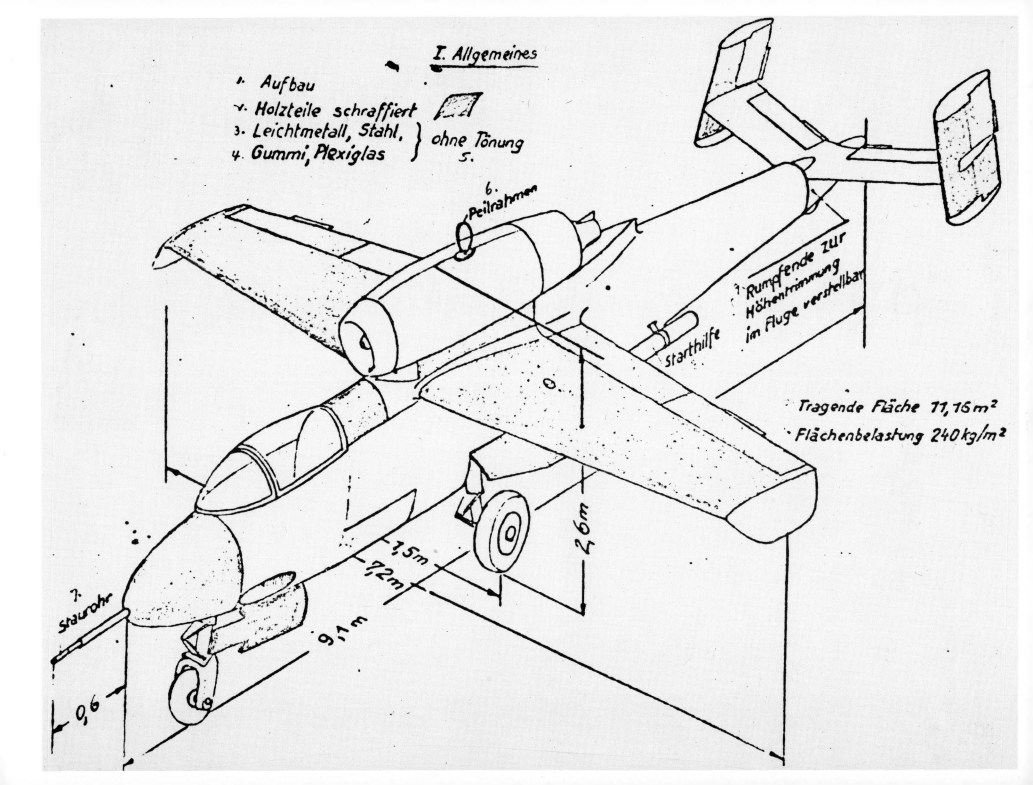

I. Allgemeines

1. Aufbau
2. Holzteile schraffiert
3. Leichtmetall, Stahl,
4. Gummi, Plexiglas
} ohne Tönung
5.

6. Peilrahmen

7. Staurohr

Rumpfende zur Höhentrimmung im Fluge verstellbar

Starthilfe

Tragende Fläche 11,16 m²

Flächenbelastung 240 kg/m²

0,6

9,1 m

7,2 m

1,5 m

2,6 m

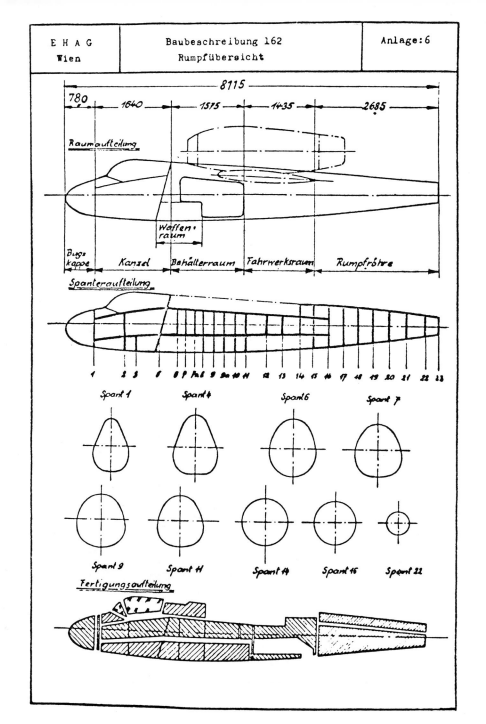

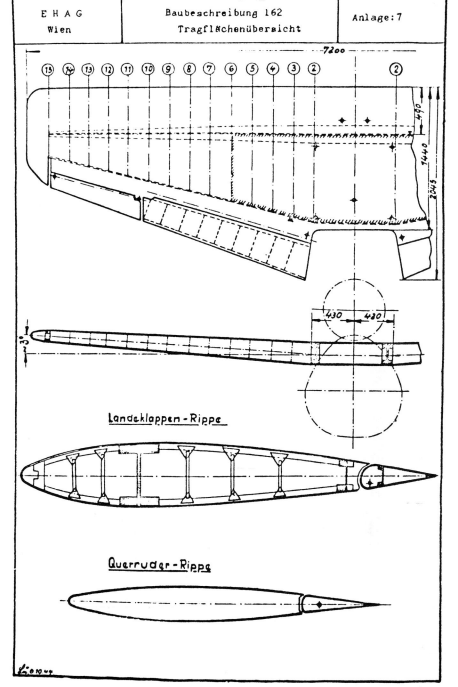

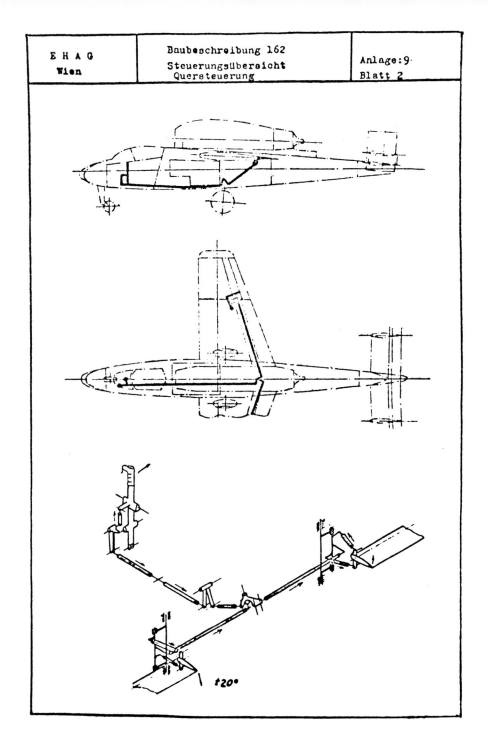

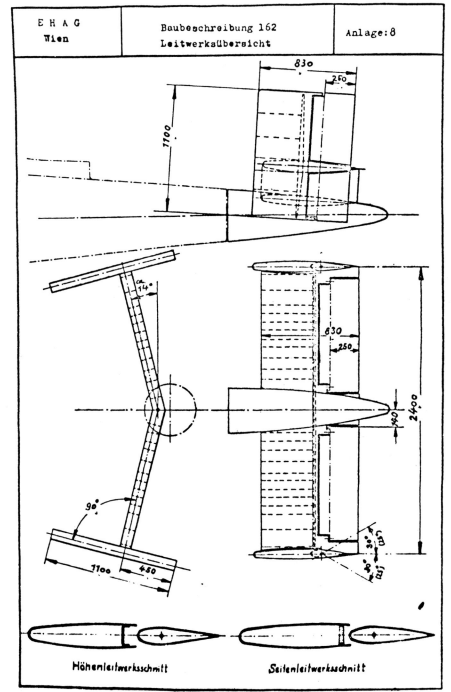

Höhenleitwerksschnitt   Seitenleitwerksschnitt

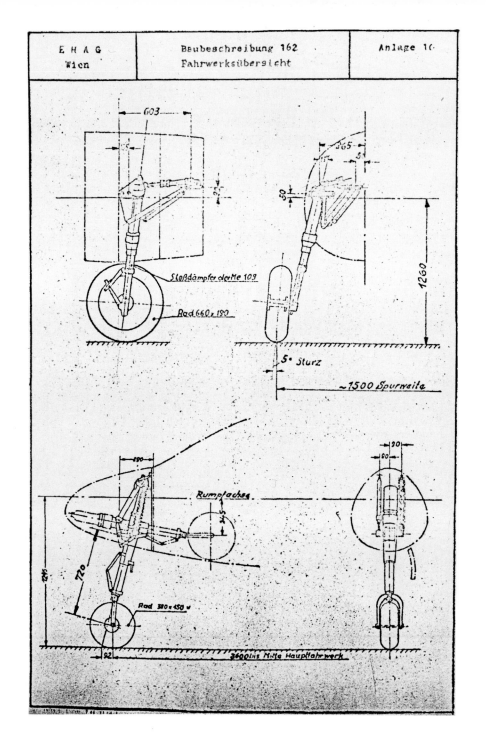

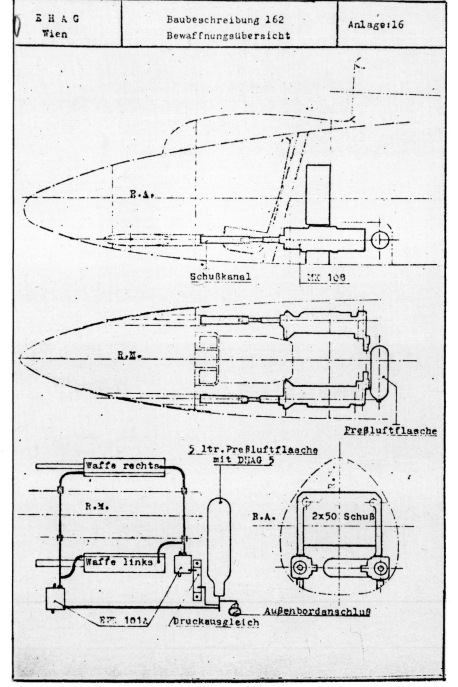

18

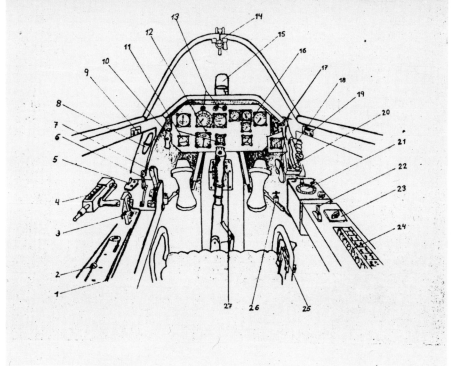

1. Jato jettison
2. Yaw trim
3. Landing gear switch
4. Pitch trim
5. Jato ignition
6. Fire extinguisher lever
7. Throttle
8. Parking brake
9. Gear indicator light, left
10. Flaps, hand pump
11. Navigational instruments
12. Flight instruments
13. Pitot tube and gun indicator lights
14. Canopy latch
15. Gunsight
16. Engine instruments
17. Oxygen system
18. Flare pistol
19. Gear indicator light, right
20. FuG 25 a operating device

21. FuG 24 radio receiver
22. Starter toggle
23. Variable jet toggle
24. Fuses
25. Ejection seat activation
26. Pedal adjustment
27. Nosewheel peep window

Fuses:
Battery
Fuel pump
Weapons, Revi gunsight
Pitot tube, heat
Ignition and instrument systems
Turn and bank indicator, Jato rockets
Variable jet
FuG 24
Fug 25 a
Starter

View of the He 162's instrument panel and joystick.

Above: One of the first production line aircraft in flight.　　　　Right side: He 162 A-2, and below and He 162 on approach to a landing.

He 162 A-2, serial numbers 120230 (foreground) and 120233 after their transfer to England.

He 162 A-2 serial number 120230 still in England.

Left and right below: During restoration in the U.S., factory serial number 120230 received a tail section with the number 120222. The reason is not known.

Sectional photos of the He 162 A-2, serial number 120077 at the time located at the Air Museum, Ontario Airfield (near Los Angeles) taken in 1966 by the Author. Above left: engine, above right: nose and cockpit, below left, exhaust gas port on the engine, below right, emblem of III/JG 27.

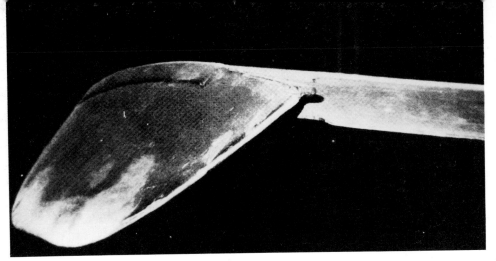

Further sectional photos of serial number 120077:

Above left: tail assembly junction
Above right: wing tip
Lower left: left side of pilot seat
Lower right: instrument panel

This He 162 A-2, probably serial number 300027, was found by U.S. troops on the Junkers factory airfield between Strassfurt and Bernbug.

Front view of He 162 A-2 serial number 120222.

Left: He 162 A-2 parked on the edge of an airfield.
Above: *Oberstleutnant* Heinz Bär was chief of the He 162 testing team. Finishing the war with 220 aerial victories, he died in a crash near Braunschweig on April 28, 1957.

Left: *Hauptmann* P.H. Dähne, commander of II/JG 1, suffered a fatal crash in a He 162 on April 24, 1945 after approximately 100 aerial victories.

Right: Walther Dahl, 128 victories, flew the He 162 and found the flight characteristics to be pleasing.

after staging out of Kirchheim-Teck with the He 162. *Oberstleutnant* Bär then went from Lechfeld to Jagdverband 44, which was commanded by *General* Galland. Galland, by the way, declined the *Volksjäger*. However, Gollob and Dahl flew it in Vienna-Schwechat and had favorable reactions to it.

February 6 saw the beginning of the rearming of I/JG 1 to the He 162 in Parchim. At this point in time the *Gruppe* was only at the strength of a *Staffel*. On February 7th, the last Fw 190's were stationed at Usedom airfield at Garz. Only a few low-level attacks against english units were flown from there. On 9 February, the first He 162's arrived at Parchim from Rostock together with *Major* Richter from the Rechlin testing facility and three flight engineers. Assignment of the flight and ground personnel was accomplished from then until March 31, 1945. The confusion in the Luftwaffe's already dissolving chain of command led to a neverending series of deployment orders: from Parchim to Köthen, from there back to Parchim, then to Ludwigslust, to Husum and finally to Leck in Holstein, where the *Gruppe* came under the leadership of *Oberleutnant* Demuth on 16 April 1945. Although there were encounters with Allied aircraft on the way from Husum to Leck, any combat engagements, as ordered by the *I Jagdkorps*, were to be avoided by utilizing the superior speed of 800 km/h.

In the meantime, the rearming of II/JG 1 had also been completed.

Above: *Oberst* Gordon M. Gollob, the last *Inspekteur der Jagdflieger*, 150 victories, flew the He 162 along with *Oberst* Dahl in Lechfeld and also found its handling characteristics pleasing.

Right: Aircraft of I and II/JG 1 on display in Leck/Holstein in May of 1945.

In early 1945, due to the backlog of BMW engines, consideration was also given to outfitting the He 162 with Argus pulse jets, the engine for the V-1. Thus the He 162 A-10 (left) and A-11 came into being. The A-10 had two Argus As 014 thruster rockets, while the A-11 had the more powerful As 044. An A-10 (M 42) flew at the end of March 1945 in Bad Gandersheim.

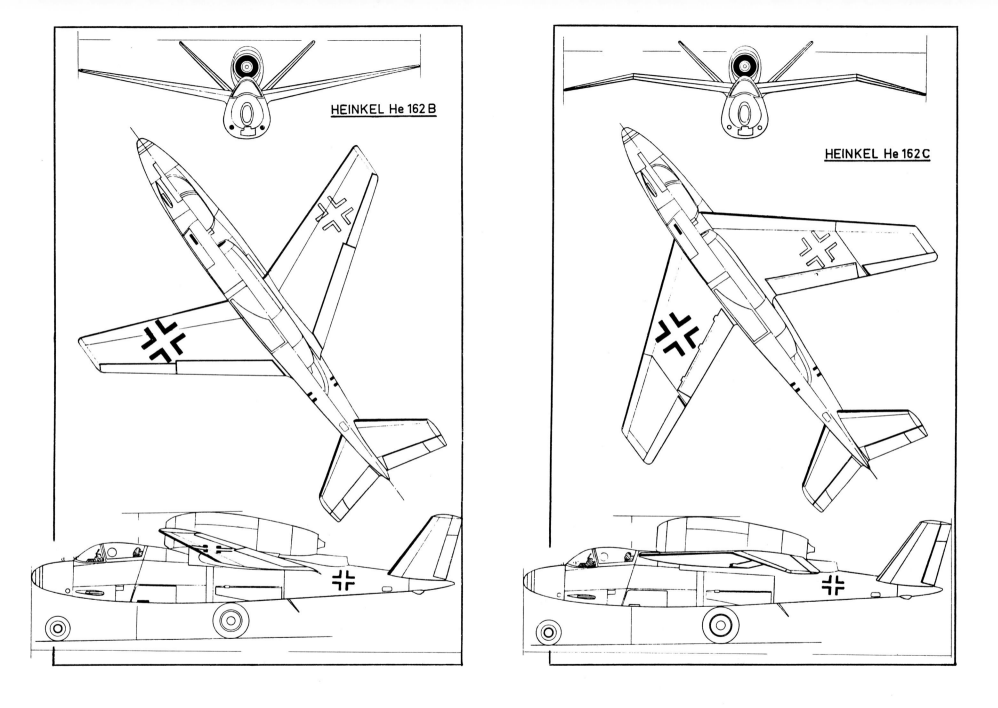

HEINKEL He 162 B

HEINKEL He 162 C

The **B** and **C** versions of the He 162 created in 1945 remained projects only.

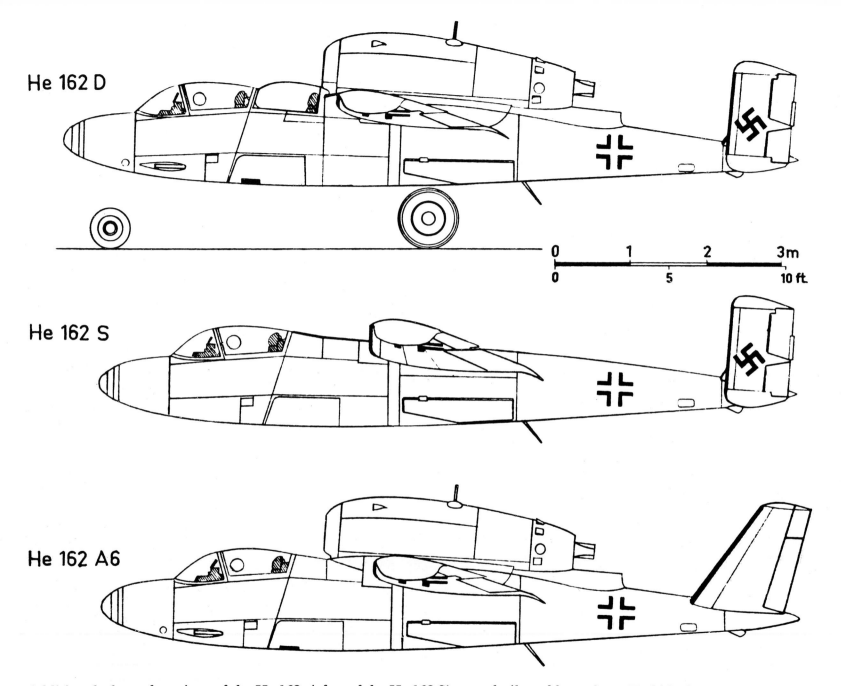

He 162 D

He 162 S

He 162 A6

Additional planned versions of the He 162. A few of the He 162 S's were built and brought to Trebbin for Hitler Youth pilot training.

He 162 A-2 of I and II/JG 1 in Leck/Holstein, May 1945.

Heinkel He 162 A-2, serial number 120074 of I/JG 1. Standing at the tail: *Oberleutnant* Demuth in Leck, May 1945 (15 victories).

It was under the leadership of *Hauptmann* Dähme, who had received the Knights' Cross in April 1944 after his 74th aerial victory and had taken over the *Gruppe* at the end of February. Dähne suffered a fatal crash in an He 162 on April 24, 1945 near Warnemünde. After Dähne's death, *Major* Zober assumed command of the II/JG 1. On May 3, 1945 the *Gruppe* then transferred to Leck together with the *Geschwader* staff and *Oberst* Ihlefeld. The *Geschwader* was organized as follows:

Staff: Kommodore Oberst Ihlefeld
I Gruppe: Major Werner Zober
  1st Staffel: Hptm. Heinz Kü"nnecke
  2nd Staffel: Hptm. Wolfgang Ludewig
  3rd Staffel: Oblt. Emil Demuth
II Gruppe: Hptm. Rahe
  4th Staffel: Hptm. Fallowitsch
  5th Staffel: Hptm. Bergholz
  6th Staffel: Oblt. Zipprecht

Pilot training was conducted in Parchim. Basically, it consisted of a quick familiarization of Fw 190 or Bf 109 pilots with the He 162. There were no two-seat training aircraft available. As an example of operating instructions, pilots were familiarized with all required control positions on the ground. The pilot had to have complete mastery of his aircraft after only 20 minutes in the air!

The first combat involvement of the He 162 was, so far as is known, conducted by I/JG 1 on April 26, 1945. The mission: engagement of enemy low-flying aircraft. During this mission, *Unteroffizier* Rechenbach achieved JG 1's first victory with the He 162. Presumably, *Oberst* Ihlefeld had already achieved the very first victory with an He 162, as mentioned, over Lechfeld. *Unteroffizier*

Oberst Herbert Ihlefeld, the Kommodore of the only He 162 fighter *Geschwader*, JG 1, approximately 150 victories.

Rechenbach was probably killed on April 26, 1945. Two comrades witnessed his victory: *Oberleutnant* Demuth and *Stabsintendant* Siegfried.

Leutnant Rudi Schmitt of I/JG 1 achieved another victory on 4 May 1945 when he succeeded in shooting down a Hawker "Typhoon." Despite the fact that neither of these victories could be officially confirmed due to conditions at the time, both victories were confirmed by eyewitnesses.

Then came the quick and bitter end. On May 4th, *Major* Zober could still report fifty combat ready He 162 A-2's in JG 1. On the following day, the cease fire went into effect at 0800, as ordered by *Luftflotte Mitte*. On May 4th 1945, at the headquarters of British Field Marshal Montgomery in Lüneberge Heide, *Generaladmiral* von Frieburg signed the terms of capitulation of all German armed forces in Holland, northwestern Germany, and Denmark.

Explosives had been installed into those He 162's still on hand. *Luftflotte Mitte* ordered that, in accordance with the conditions of surrender, all the aircraft were to be handed over undamaged, and the explosives were removed by midnight. On May 6th, British tanks rolled onto Lech airfield. Officers and men cleaned out the files and spent the following weeks in the Schmörholm barracks. Two days later, two teams arrived — one British and one American. They seized JG 1's aircraft.

Officer of JG 1 await the english transfer team. Above, from left, *Hauptmann* Ludewig, 2/JG 1, *Major* Zober, I/JG 1, *Hauptmann* Künnecke, 1/JG 1 and *Oberleutnant* Demuth, 3/JG 1.

Then, on May 6, 1945 British tanks rolled onto the *Jagdgeschwader 1* airfield. Just prior to this the men of JG 1 had been discussing just what to expect from the British once the transfer of aircraft was complete.

This is how the victors discovered the *Volksjäger* on many airfields: above left: M 20, serial number 220003, maiden flight on February 10, 1945, partly destroyed on February 25 1945. Above right: M 20 from behind, in front of it is M 23, serial number 220006. Below left: M 20 from behind, below right: M 23. These photographs came from the Munich-Riem airfield.

This He 162 had been parked due to its lack of an engine.

The Allies were keenly interested in obtaining the German jet fighter aircraft. One American General later publicly admitted that the developmental work done by the Germans in the area of jet aircraft and rockets saved the Allies 20 years of research.

As such, there are fine examples of the Heinkel He 162 available today. They are predominantly He 162 A-2's of the 120 series. They were:

Werknr.	as Royal Air Force	to England
120021	AM 58	
120086	AM 60	
120072	AM 61	
129976		to Canada
120097	AM 64	to England
120227	AM 65	
120091	AM 66	
530552	AM 67	
?	from U.S. Technical Intelligence	to France
120017	as U.S. T2-494	to the U.S.
120222	U.S. T2-504	
120077	U.S. T2-489	

British spoils: Above He 162 A-2 serial number 120097 in September 1945 at Farnborough. Below: Serial number 120086 in Hyde Park, London.

Aircraft number 120222 is located in the Smithsonian Institution in Washington D.C. Serial number 120077 is in the Ontario Air Museum in California (currently the "Planes of Fame" Museum in Chino, California). One aircraft is now in the Musee de l'Air in France. Serial number 120086 was displayed as the first He 162 at Hyde Park in 1945. 120097 was thoroughly tested at Farnborough. 120227 is now at the R.A.F College in Crawell and 530552 at R.A.F. Station Colerne.

An He 162 formerly of JG 1 with U.S. markings T2-489. This is actually serial number 120077. The aircraft was tested extensively by the U.S. Air Force, as is shown in the photo. This is the same aircraft viewed by the author in 1967 and which is now on display in Ed Maloney's "Planes of Fame" museum in Chino, California.

He 162 A-2, serial number 120227, taken in August 1971 at RAF Chivenor air base.

An He 162, also of JG 1, is now in the collection of the Imperial War Museum in London. Behind it is a De Havilland DH 9 from World War I.

He 162 A-2, serial number 120223, also a JG 1 aircraft, is now the the Musee de l'Air in Paris.

In 1963, a member of the Heinkel Firm at Stuttgart-Zuffenhausen, Armin Kerle, built a model of the He 162 at the request of Ernst Heinkel. The model is extremely accurate as it was built according to actual factory blueprints.

Photos of the nose, nosewheel and main gear of this
model show all the details to accurate.

When viewing the model from this perspective, one believes they are watching a real He 162 coming in for a landing.

TECHNICAL DATA

	He 162 A-1	He 162 A-10	He 162 A-11
Crew	one	one	one
Engine	BMW 003E	AS-014	AS-044
Power	920kp	335kp (x2)	500kp
Fuel weight	755 kg	1,400 kg	1,100 kg
Wingspan	7.3 meters	7.2 meters	7.2 meters
Length	9.05 meters	9.05 meters	9.05 meters
Height	2.6 meters	2.6 meters	2.6 meters
Wing area	11.16m	11.16m	11.16m
Empty weight	1,663kg	1,632kg	1,674kg
Max speed			
(sea level)	790 km/h	712 km/h	810 km/h
(6000 meters)	620 km/h	590 km/h	712 km/h
(11000 meters)	975 km/h	unknown	unknown
Max range with full throttle			
(sea level)	390 km	320 km	370 km
(6000 meters)	620 km	380 km	415 km
(11000 meters)	975 km	unknown	unknown
Takeoff roll	980 meters	525 meters	525 meters
Max altitude	8000 meters	6500 meters	8000 meters
Armament	2 MK 108	2 MK 108	2 MK 108
Ammunition	50 rounds	50 rounds	50 rounds